NAVIGAT... DEMENTIA CARE

Practical Strategies for Coping with the Challenges of Dementia Care

EMILY BAKER

Copyright © 2023 by Emily Baker

This book is a labor of love and the result of countless hours of research and dedication. It is the author's hope that the information contained within these pages will inspire and enlighten readers, and contribute to a better understanding of Dementia Care.

TABLE OF CONTENTS

NAVIGATING DEMENTIA CARE

INTRODUCTION

As a caregiver for my father, who was diagnosed with dementia, I embarked on a journey that was both challenging and rewarding. It was a journey that required me to learn how to navigate the complex landscape of dementia care, and one that ultimately led me to write this book.

When my father was first diagnosed with dementia, I had no idea what to expect. I had heard of dementia, of course, but I knew very little about it. As the weeks and months went by, however, I began to realize just how devastating this disease could be. I watched as my father struggled to remember things that had once been second nature to him, and I saw how frustrated he became when he couldn't express himself as he wanted to.

But as difficult as it was to watch my father's decline, I also saw how much he appreciated the care and support that my family and I provided. I saw how a simple smile or a kind word could brighten his day, and I witnessed how important it was to him that we were there for him, no matter what.

As a caregiver, I quickly realized that I needed to educate myself about dementia and how to provide the best care possible for my father. I read everything I could find on the subject, attended support groups, and sought advice from medical professionals. I also learned through trial and error, as I tried different strategies and techniques to help my father manage his symptoms and maintain his quality of life.

Through it all, I kept a journal of my experiences as a caregiver, recording my thoughts, feelings, and observations. As I wrote, I began to see patterns emerging and realized that certain strategies and approaches were particularly effective for my father. I also saw how my own experiences and emotions as a caregiver were universal and how they could be helpful to others going through similar situations.

That's why I decided to write this book, Navigating Dementia Care. It is a guide for caregivers, written from the perspective of someone who has been there. It provides practical advice and strategies for managing the many challenges of dementia care, as well as insights into the emotional journey of caregiving.

Whether you're just starting out on the journey of dementia care or you've been caring for a loved one for years, this book will help you navigate the ups and downs, providing you with the knowledge, skills, and support you need to provide the best possible care for your loved one, while also taking care of yourself.

In the pages of this book, you'll find practical tips on how to communicate with someone with dementia, how to manage difficult behaviors, and how to provide meaningful activities and engagement. You'll also learn about the different stages of dementia and what to expect at each stage, as well as tips for managing the various symptoms that may arise.

However, this book offers more than just practical advice. It's also a tribute to the love and dedication that caregivers bring to their roles. It's a reminder that even amid the challenges and difficulties of dementia care, there is hope, there is joy, and there is love.

As you read this book, I hope you'll feel a sense of solidarity and support, knowing that you're not alone on this journey. I hope you'll feel empowered with new knowledge and skills to help you provide the best possible care for your loved one. And I hope you'll find comfort in the knowledge that the love and care you provide to your loved one is invaluable and truly makes a difference.

CHAPTER ONE

Understanding Dementia

This chapter gives a thorough overview of dementia, including what it is, the many varieties of dementia, its causes and risk factors, symptoms, and phases. For caregivers and healthcare workers who work with people living with dementia, this chapter serves as a foundational chapter by offering crucial information.

Understanding the fundamentals of dementia will help caregivers give dementia patients the proper care and assistance they need, enhancing their quality of life and general well-being. The chapter is meant to serve as a solid foundation for the remainder of the book, which focuses on doable solutions to dementia care's difficulties.

Definition of Dementia

Dementia is a medical condition characterized by a decline in cognitive function, which includes problems with memory, thinking, and reasoning. This decline is severe enough to interfere with daily activities and can lead to a loss of independence. Dementia can be caused by various underlying conditions, such as Alzheimer's disease, vascular disease, or Parkinson's disease, among others.

Symptoms of dementia may include memory loss, difficulty communicating, disorientation, changes in mood or behavior, and difficulty with daily tasks. Although there is no known cure for dementia, various treatments are accessible that can aid in managing symptoms and enhancing the individual's quality of life.

Types of Dementia

Alzheimer's Disease

The most prevalent kind of dementia, accounting for 60 to 80 percent of all cases, is Alzheimer's disease. It is a chronic and irreversible brain condition that has an impact on cognition, behavior, and memory. The buildup of beta-amyloid and tau proteins in the brain, which results in the loss of brain cells and a reduction in cognitive function, is what causes Alzheimer's disease. Memory loss is usually the first sign of Alzheimer's disease, which can progress to include issues with language, judgment, and daily functioning.

In the early stages of Alzheimer's disease, the individual may have trouble recalling recent conversations or events, misplace objects, or struggle to complete routine chores. People may struggle with language, go through mood and behavior changes, and struggle with mobility and coordination as the illness worsens. Those with advanced Alzheimer's disease may lose their ability to converse or carry out even the most basic duties, necessitating full-time care.

Alzheimer's disease does not presently have a cure, however drugs like cholinesterase inhibitors and memantine can help control the symptoms and delay the illness's progression. The quality of life for people with Alzheimer's disease and their caregivers may be enhanced by lifestyle changes like consistent exercise, a nutritious diet, and social interaction.

Vascular Dementia

Vascular dementia is a type of cognitive impairment that occurs due to a decreased blood flow to the brain, causing brain cells to die and leading to a decline in cognitive function. The brain requires a continuous supply of oxygen and nutrients through blood flow to function properly. When the blood flow is restricted, it can cause damage or death of the brain cells, resulting in a variety of symptoms associated with vascular dementia.

There are various factors that can cause reduced blood flow to the brain, such as stroke, high blood pressure, or atherosclerosis, which is a buildup of plaque in the arteries. A stroke can happen when the blood flow to the brain is blocked or interrupted, resulting in brain cell death. High blood pressure can also cause damage to the blood vessels in the brain over time, leading to a decrease in blood flow. Atherosclerosis can also cause a reduction in blood flow by narrowing the arteries that supply blood to the brain.

Vascular dementia symptoms can vary, depending on the extent and location of the brain damage. Some common symptoms include difficulties with memory, problem-solving, and communication. Individuals with vascular dementia may experience difficulty remembering recent events or maintaining attention during tasks. They may also have difficulty organizing and planning tasks or finding the right words to express themselves. In some cases, individuals with vascular dementia may also exhibit changes in mood and behavior, such as depression, anxiety, or apathy.

Diagnosing vascular dementia typically involves a comprehensive evaluation of an individual's medical history, in addition to physical and neurological exams. Doctors may also use imaging tests, such as MRI or CT scans, to detect any brain changes that are consistent with vascular dementia.

Treatment for vascular dementia may involve managing the underlying conditions that caused the reduction in blood flow to the brain. For example, medications may be prescribed to manage high blood pressure or to reduce the risk of blood clots. In some cases, surgical procedures may be recommended to restore blood flow to the brain. Additionally, medications can be prescribed to manage symptoms and improve blood flow to the brain, although there is no known cure for vascular dementia.

Lewy Body Dementia

Lewy Body Dementia (LBD) is a form of dementia that occurs due to the presence of Lewy bodies, abnormal protein deposits in the brain that disrupt normal brain function. This leads to a progressive decline in cognitive, movement, and behavioral abilities.

LBD can be categorized into two types: Dementia with Lewy bodies (DLB) and Parkinson's disease dementia (PDD). DLB is characterized by cognitive decline, visual hallucinations, and movement problems, while PDD involves both Parkinson's disease symptoms and cognitive decline.

The cause of LBD is not yet fully understood, but it is believed to be related to a combination of genetic and environmental factors. LBD is more common in people over the age of 60.

Early signs of LBD can include problems with attention and visual perception, visual hallucinations, and REM sleep behavior disorder. Later symptoms may include memory loss, movement problems, and changes in behavior and mood.

Diagnosing LBD can be challenging due to the overlapping symptoms with other types of dementia and movement disorders. A thorough evaluation, including medical history, physical and neurological exams, and imaging tests, may be used to diagnose LBD.

There is currently no cure for LBD, but medications can be prescribed to manage the symptoms, such as cognitive decline and movement problems. Caregiver support and education can also help manage the challenges associated with LBD.

Frontotemporal Dementia

Frontotemporal dementia (FTD) is a type of dementia that affects the frontal and temporal lobes of the brain, which are responsible for regulating behavior, emotions, and language. This type of dementia is caused by degeneration of the nerve cells in these areas of the brain, leading to a decline in cognitive abilities and changes in behavior and personality.

FTD can be classified into three subtypes based on the area of the brain that is affected: behavioral variant FTD (bvFTD), semantic dementia, and progressive nonfluent aphasia. Each subtype has unique symptoms and characteristics.

The behavioral variant of FTD is the most common subtype and is characterized by changes in personality, behavior, and emotional regulation. Individuals with bvFTD may experience a loss of empathy, impulsivity, lack of judgment, and social disinhibition.

Semantic dementia is characterized by a loss of language and word comprehension, making it difficult for individuals to communicate effectively. This subtype of FTD typically affects the left side of the brain and can lead to the loss of understanding of words and concepts.

Progressive nonfluent aphasia is characterized by difficulties with language production and may affect the ability to speak, write, and understand language. This subtype of FTD is typically caused by degeneration of the left side of the brain.

Diagnosing FTD can be challenging, as the symptoms can be similar to other types of dementia and mental health conditions. A comprehensive evaluation, including medical history, physical and neurological exams, and imaging tests, may be used to diagnose FTD.

While there is no known cure for Frontotemporal Dementia (FTD), the focus of treatment is on managing symptoms and enhancing the patient's quality of life. Medications can be prescribed to manage symptoms such as depression and anxiety, and speech therapy and behavioral interventions can be beneficial for individuals with FTD.

Mixed Dementia

A person with mixed dementia has two or more kinds of dementia concurrently, frequently Alzheimer's disease and vascular dementia. Depending on the types of dementia present, mixed dementia symptoms might vary, but they commonly include memory loss, language problems, and alterations in mood and behavior.

Given that its symptoms often resemble those of other varieties of dementia, mixed dementia can be difficult to diagnose. Therapy for mixed dementia could involve taking medications to control underlying diseases like hypertension and changing one's lifestyle to lower the risk of having more strokes. In some situations, a combination of drugs may be used to treat the symptoms of both vascular dementia and Alzheimer's disease.

Knowing the various forms of dementia can make it easier for patients and their caregivers to deal with the difficulties of dementia care. It is crucial to remember that every individual with dementia is distinct and may experience symptoms in a variety of ways. It is frequently required to have a thorough evaluation by a medical specialist to determine the type of dementia and create an effective treatment strategy.

Causes and Risk Factors

A wide number of causes and risk factors can contribute to dementia, which is a complex disorder. Researchers have found several characteristics that can raise a person's risk of acquiring dementia, even though the precise origins of the disorder are not yet entirely understood. Individuals and their carers should be aware of these causes and risk factors as it can help them take proactive measures to lower their risk of dementia and better manage the condition.

Age: The primary factor that increases the chances of developing dementia is advancing age. Although dementia can affect anyone of any age, the majority of instances affect those over the age of 65. Dementia is not a typical aspect of the aging process, even though age-related changes in the brain are a regular element of aging.

Genetics: Dementia development may also be influenced by genetics. People may be more likely to develop dementia themselves if there is a family history of the disease. Some genes, such as the APOE 4 gene for Alzheimer's disease, have been found to enhance the likelihood of getting some types of dementia.

Lifestyle factors: Dementia risk can also be increased by lifestyle choices. A sedentary lifestyle, heavy drinking, and smoking have all been linked to an increased risk of dementia, according to research. On the other hand, a balanced diet, frequent exercise, and mental stimulation can all help lower the risk of dementia.

Head injuries: The likelihood of dementia emerging later in life has been linked to head traumas, particularly those that cause loss of consciousness. Both a single serious head injury as well as repeated minor head injuries, such as those sustained in contact sports like football, are covered by this. Other risk factors, such as genetics and age, can further raise the likelihood of dementia following a head injury.

Medical conditions: Dementia risk can be increased by medical diseases such as diabetes, high cholesterol, and hypertension. These disorders can harm the blood arteries in the brain, which can reduce oxygen and blood flow to the brain and has been linked to dementia. Moreover, vascular dementia may be more likely to develop in people with a history of stroke or cardiovascular illness.

Neurological disorders: Dementia risk can also be increased by neurological conditions including Parkinson's disease and Huntington's disease. Dementia may develop as a result of several conditions harming the brain cells necessary for cognitive function. Moreover, dementia risk may be higher in people with a history of epilepsy or multiple sclerosis.

Environmental factors: A higher incidence of dementia has been connected to exposure to specific environmental pollutants. For instance, prolonged exposure to heavy metals like lead and mercury can harm the brain and increase the risk of developing dementia. The incidence of dementia has also been linked to pesticides and other chemicals used in industry and agriculture. Also linked to an increased incidence of dementia is air pollution.

It is crucial to remember that many of these risk factors are adjustable, which enables people to adopt preventative measures to lower their chance of dementia. For instance, giving up smoking, consuming less alcohol, and engaging in more physical activity can all help lower the risk of dementia. Moreover, controlling medical disorders like diabetes and hypertension can lower the risk of acquiring dementia.

In conclusion, although the precise causes of dementia are not entirely understood, researchers have found several risk factors that can raise a person's risk of getting the disorder. People with dementia and those who care for them can lower the risk of dementia by being aware of these risk factors and taking proactive measures to better manage the condition. In addition to managing existing medical illnesses and avoiding environmental contaminants, this may entail making changes to one's way of life, such as engaging in regular exercise and eating a balanced diet.

Symptoms of Dementia

Cognitive function, memory, and behavior all deteriorate as a result of dementia, a degenerative disorder that damages the brain. Depending on the type of dementia and the particular circumstances of each person, the signs and stages of dementia might vary greatly. There are, however, several widespread signs and stages that are frequently linked to dementia.

Symptoms

Memory loss: One of the most prevalent signs of dementia is memory loss. This can involve having trouble recalling recent events, losing track of names or faces, asking the same questions, or telling the same stories repeatedly.

Communication problems: Dementia patients may find it challenging to communicate with others. This can involve having trouble putting your thoughts into words, having trouble following a discussion, or having issues with reading and writing.

Difficulty with daily tasks: It might be difficult for people with dementia to carry out daily duties like cooking, cleaning, or getting dressed. This may be brought on by difficulties with problem-solving and planning, as well as a loss in motor skills.

Changes in behavior: Dementia patients may behave differently, showing signs of agitation, hostility, and impatience. They could also go through despair, apathy, or anxiousness.

Confusion and disorientation: People with dementia may experience confusion and disorientation, especially in new settings or circumstances. Even in places they are familiar with, they could get lost or confused.

Stages of Dementia

The different stages of dementia can be categorized into three main groups: early stage, middle stage, and late stage. During the early stage, people with dementia may exhibit mild cognitive impairment, such as forgetfulness and difficulty with concentration. They may also have difficulty finding the right words when communicating, experience mood swings, and have trouble with tasks that require planning and organization.

As the disease progresses to the middle stage, symptoms become more noticeable. People with dementia may experience confusion, forgetfulness, and difficulty with activities of daily living, such as dressing and bathing. They may also experience changes in personality and behavior, including agitation, aggression, and wandering. In addition, they may have difficulty recognizing familiar faces and objects and have trouble with spatial awareness.

In the late stage of dementia, individuals may lose the ability to communicate effectively and may be unable to recognize family members and caregivers. They may require assistance with all activities of daily living, including eating, drinking, and using the bathroom. People in the late stage of dementia may also experience difficulty with swallowing, which can lead to weight loss and malnutrition. Furthermore, they may be more prone to infections, such as pneumonia, due to a weakened immune system.

It is important to bear in mind that dementia progression is not the same for everyone and may vary from person to person. Each individual may exhibit different symptoms or progress through the stages of the disease at different rates. Some may experience rapid decline, while others may have a slower progression of the disease.

CHAPTER TWO

Diagnosis and Treatment of Dementia

Dementia is a complex disorder that requires precise diagnosis and efficient treatment to improve the quality of life for patients and their caregivers. The method of diagnosing dementia, as well as the various tests and evaluations that healthcare professionals employ, will be covered in this chapter. We will also go over the different types of treatments that are available, such as drugs, counseling, and lifestyle modifications.

Caregivers and loved ones can more effectively support persons with dementia and assist in managing their symptoms by being aware of the diagnostic and treatment process.

Diagnosis Process

Dementia diagnosis can be a difficult process that requires numerous evaluations and tests. To ensure that the proper care and treatment can be given, a precise diagnosis of dementia is crucial. The steps in the dementia diagnosis procedure are as follows:

Medical History and Physical Examination: Reviewing the patient's medical history and performing a physical examination are frequently the first steps in dementia diagnosis. The patient's symptoms and medical history, including any drugs they may be taking, previous illnesses, and any family history of dementia, will be discussed with the patient and their family members by the healthcare provider. To rule out any additional potential reasons for cognitive impairment, such as a brain tumor, stroke, or infection, they will also do a physical examination.

Cognitive and Neuropsychological Testing: A battery of tests used in cognitive and neuropsychological evaluations evaluates memory, attention, language, problem-solving, and other cognitive abilities. These examinations can aid in determining the kind of dementia as well as the degree and severity of cognitive impairment. The Mini-Mental State Examination (MMSE), the Montreal Cognitive Assessment (MoCA), and the Neuropsychological Test Battery are a few examples of the tests that can be used.

Imaging Tests: Imaging procedures like computed tomography (CT) and magnetic resonance imaging (MRI) scans can assist detect changes in the brain that could be related to dementia, such as shrinkage or the development of aberrant protein deposits. Other potential causes of cognitive impairment, such as a brain tumor, can be ruled out with the aid of these tests.

Laboratory Tests: Other potential reasons for cognitive impairment, such as thyroid dysfunction or vitamin shortages, can be ruled out through laboratory procedures including blood tests.

Moreover, blood testing can be performed to look for genetic indicators linked to certain forms of dementia, like familial Alzheimer's disease.

Specialist Referral: A healthcare provider may occasionally refer a patient to a specialist for additional assessment and diagnosis, such as a neurologist or geriatric psychiatrist. To support a diagnosis and assist in choosing the most appropriate treatments, these specialists can do more thorough tests and assessments.

Diagnostic Criteria: Diagnostic criteria, such as those included in the Diagnostic and Statistical Manual of Mental Disorders (DSM-5) or the International Classification of Diseases, are commonly used to make the diagnosis of dementia (ICD-11). The patient's cognitive, behavioral, and functional capacities are taken into consideration by these criteria.

Overall, diagnosing dementia is a thorough review that includes a variety of evaluations and testing. A proper diagnosis can ensure that the patient receives the right care and treatment, as well as help caretakers make plans. It is crucial to remember that the diagnosing procedure may be difficult and time-consuming, therefore persistence and patience are essential.

Treatment Options

While there is no known cure for the majority of dementias, there are some therapeutic options that can help patients and their caregivers live more comfortably and control symptoms. The dementia treatment strategy is often individualized based on the patient's symptoms, medical history, and disease stage. The following are some dementia treatments:

Medications

The cognitive and behavioral signs of dementia can be controlled with medication. In patients with mild to severe Alzheimer's disease, cholinesterase inhibitors such as donepezil, rivastigmine, and galantamine can enhance cognitive performance and halt the progression of symptoms. These drugs work by raising the levels of acetylcholine, a chemical messenger important for cognitive function, in the brain. Another drug that can be used to treat mild to severe Alzheimer's disease is memantine. This drug affects learning and memory by controlling the activity of glutamate, a different chemical messenger in the brain.

Treatment for behavioral symptoms like sadness, anxiety, agitation, and aggression can also involve the use of antidepressants and antipsychotics. However, due to possible side effects, these drugs should be used with caution.

Non-Pharmacological Therapies

For dementia patients, non-pharmacological treatments can be successful in reducing symptoms and enhancing quality of life. Examples include

Cognitive stimulation therapy: This treatment entails several structured exercises that are meant to boost cognitive function and enhance memory, attention, and communication abilities. The exercises may consist of memory exercises, games, and puzzles.

Reminiscence therapy: This therapy involves talking about the patient's past encounters and memories, which can lift their spirits and calm them down. Those with mid-stage dementia may benefit the most from this treatment.

Music therapy: Music therapy involves either listening to or performing music, which can assist to lessen restlessness, depression, and anxiety. Music can also be used to arouse emotions and memories.

Art therapy: This involves doing creative things like painting or drawing, which can help lift your mood and calm you down. Self-expression and communication can also be fostered through art therapy.

Lifestyle Changes

Lifestyle changes can also help dementia people manage their symptoms and live better. Examples include:

Regular exercise: Exercise can lower the risk of falling and enhance physical and cognitive performance. With dementia sufferers, exercise can also aid with despair and anxiety reduction.

Healthy diet: Eating healthily can lower the chance of developing diseases like diabetes and heart disease while also enhancing physical and cognitive function. It is advised to eat a diet high in fruits, vegetables, whole grains, and lean protein.

Socialization: Being socially active can lift your spirits and lessen feelings of loneliness and seclusion. Group outings, volunteering, and spending time with friends and family are all positive activities.

Sleep: Having regular sleep patterns might enhance cognitive performance and lessen agitation. It can be beneficial to create a relaxing environment for sleeping, keep a regular sleep pattern, and abstain from coffee and alcohol before bed.

Support for Caregivers: For caregivers to manage the physical, emotional, and financial demands of caregiving, they must receive the assistance and resources they need. Carers play a significant role in the treatment of individuals with dementia. Counseling, short-term care, dementia care, and management training are all examples of support. It's important to encourage caregivers to get support and look after their health and well-being.

In conclusion, there are many different ways to treat dementia, including drugs, non-pharmacological therapy, dietary changes, and assistance for caregivers. For dementia patients and their carers, a multidisciplinary approach that integrates a range of therapies and methods can help manage symptoms and enhance quality of life.

Medications for dementia

The cognitive and behavioral signs of dementia can be controlled with medication. Some of the most widely prescribed drugs for dementia include the ones listed below:

Cholinesterase Inhibitors: Acetylcholine, a chemical messenger in the brain, is increased in concentration by cholinesterase inhibitors, a class of drugs. Memory, learning, and attention are some of the cognitive processes that are impacted by this chemical messenger. Donepezil, rivastigmine, and galantamine are the most often prescribed cholinesterase inhibitors.

Patients with mild to moderate Alzheimer's disease are often treated with cholinesterase inhibitors. According to studies, these drugs can enhance daily living activities, prevent the onset of more severe symptoms, and enhance cognitive function. Unfortunately, these drugs' efficacy varies from person to person and might not be effective for all people.

Memantine: Memantine is a drug that controls the function of glutamate, a chemical messenger in the brain. Glutamate is thought to contribute to the development of Alzheimer's disease and is involved in learning and memory. Those with moderate to severe Alzheimer's disease frequently receive the medication memantine.

Memantine has been proven in studies to enhance daily living activities, delay the onset of more severe symptoms, and enhance cognitive performance. Memantine's efficacy, however, may differ from person to person and may not be effective for all patients.

Antidepressants: Antidepressants can be recommended to treat depression, which is a prevalent symptom in dementia sufferers. For this reason, selective serotonin reuptake inhibitors (SSRIs) like fluoxetine, citalopram, and sertraline are frequently utilized.

Anxiety and irritation are two other symptoms that can be treated with antidepressants. Antidepressants may manage these symptoms differently for different people, so it's crucial to keep an eye out for any potential negative effects.

Antipsychotics: These can be used to treat behavioral problems like agitation, aggressiveness, and psychosis. Risperidone and olanzapine, two antipsychotic medications, are frequently taken for this reason. However, due to possible adverse effects like drowsiness, falls, and increased mortality, these drugs should be used with caution.

Due to a reduced risk of adverse effects, second-generation antipsychotics like risperidone and olanzapine are favored over first-generation antipsychotics. Antipsychotic use needs to be tailored to the person and thoroughly watched for effectiveness and negative effects.

It is significant to remember that drug therapy for dementia should be tailored to the patient's symptoms, medical history, and disease stage. Medication use should only be done with a doctor's approval, after carefully weighing the risks and advantages of the therapy. Frequent monitoring is necessary to evaluate the efficacy of drug therapy and spot any potential side effects.

Alternative Therapies

Alternative dementia treatments are non-pharmacological approaches that assist people with dementia to feel better, live better lives, and improve their quality of life. These treatments may involve a variety of activities and interventions to improve the patient's physical, cognitive, and emotional functioning. These are some complementary treatments for dementia symptoms that have shown promise:

Art therapy: With the use of art therapy, people with dementia can better express their feelings, cope with worry and depression, and lift their spirits. Art therapy is a nonverbal kind of treatment. Drawing, painting, sculpting, and other forms of creative expression can all be used in art therapy. According to studies, art therapy can enhance a person's quality of life, lessen behavioral symptoms, and boost communication in dementia patients.

Music therapy: Music-making or -listening is used as a therapeutic intervention in music therapy. It can lessen agitation, uplift mood, and improve cognitive performance. Singing, playing an instrument, or just listening to your favorite music are all acceptable forms of music therapy. According to studies, music therapy can help dementia patients with their memory recall as well as their anxiety and sadness.

Pet therapy: Interacting with trained animals is used as a type of therapy. It can enhance mood, lessen tension and anxiety, and promote social engagement. According to studies, pet therapy can improve social interactions, lessen agitation, and boost emotions of well-being in dementia patients.

Reminiscence therapy: Reminiscence therapy is a type of therapy that entails sharing and recalling old memories. It can help elevate mood, lessen anxiety and despair, and improve cognitive performance. Looking through photo albums, discussing the past, or listening to stories are all common reminiscence therapy activities. Reminiscence therapy has been found in studies to help people with dementia communicate better, manage behavioral issues, and feel better overall.

Exercise therapy: Exercise therapy uses physical activity as a type of therapy. It can assist to promote cognitive functioning, lessen behavioral problems, and improve physical functioning. Walking, cycling, or strength training are some examples of exercises that can be used as therapy. Exercise therapy has been found in studies to help people with dementia with balance, fall prevention, and overall physical functioning.

To improve overall care and the quality of life for people with dementia, complementary and alternative therapies are frequently utilized in conjunction with medicine and other traditional treatments. To make sure that any alternative therapy is secure and suitable for the patient's needs, it is crucial to speak with a healthcare practitioner before beginning it.

CHAPTER THREE

Communication Strategies for Caregivers

Caregiving for someone with dementia requires effective communication. People may have trouble communicating and understanding others as the disease worsens. Frustration, uncertainty, and loneliness may result from this. For people with dementia to feel connected and understood as well as to communicate effectively, caregivers are essential.

In this chapter, we'll look at a variety of communication techniques that family caregivers might employ to improve interactions with the people they care for.

Challenges in Communication

Caregivers may feel overwhelmed and worn out by the communication difficulties that come with caring for someone who has dementia. These difficulties can result in unpleasant interactions, misunderstandings, and uncertainty for both the caregiver and the dementia patient. They are frequently aggravating. Developing effective communication methods requires an understanding of the communication issues brought on by dementia.

Finding the appropriate words or forgetting familiar words is one of the most frequent communication difficulties for people with dementia. The person may find it difficult to fully explain their thoughts and feelings, which can lead to rambling conversations. People may repeat the same words or phrases or confuse terms as the disease worsens, which can be frustrating and make communication challenges even worse.

Understanding what others are saying might be challenging, which is another common communication obstacle for people with dementia. This may result in misunderstandings and erroneous interpretations, which may cause unpleasant interactions and dissatisfaction. Also, people with dementia may find it difficult to follow conversations or stay on topic, which can make communication difficult for carers.

When dementia worsens, people may become easily distracted or lose sight of the conversation, making it challenging to maintain communication. They might also speak incoherently or rambly, which can make it difficult for caregivers to decipher what they are trying to say. Also, people with dementia may struggle to communicate nonverbally, such as through body language or facial expressions, which can lead to misconceptions and further communication problems.

Caregivers must create successful communication plans that emphasize improving understanding, encouraging good relationships, and lowering frustration to overcome these communication difficulties. These tactics might be:

- Using concise, plain language while avoiding jargon and convoluted sentences
- Giving the person time to think about the situation and answer
- Using visual aids to support spoken communication, such as images or gestures
- Dividing information or instructions into doable, tiny steps
- Concentrating on the person's sentiments and emotions rather than the words they use in particular
- Promoting attentive listening and, when necessary, asking for clarification
- Employing positive body language and maintaining eye contact to encourage engagement and connection.

Caregivers can encourage good relationships, improve comprehension, and enhance the general quality of life for people with dementia by being aware of the communication difficulties brought on by dementia and putting appropriate communication practices into practice.

Tips for Effective Communication

It can be difficult to communicate effectively with people who have dementia, but there are several strategies that caregivers can take to improve their communication and foster positive connections. Among these strategies are:

Speak slowly and clearly: Talk slowly and clearly to help those with dementia understand what is being said. People with dementia may have trouble processing information, so it is important to speak slowly and clearly to them.

Use simple language: Avoid utilizing sophisticated words or medical jargon that can mislead the person by speaking in plain terms. To ensure understanding, use straightforward language and reiterate crucial topics.

Show respect and empathy: Respect and empathy should always be shown when speaking with someone who has dementia because they may experience frustration or confusion. Actively hear them out and respect their emotions.

Use non-verbal cues: People with dementia may find it challenging to communicate themselves verbally, but non-verbal cues like facial expressions, tone of voice, and body language can be useful for expressing meaning and feelings.

Use positive body language: Keep eye contact, smile, and use positive body language to convey interest and a sense of connection.

Focus on the individual's emotions: While talking, pay attention to the person's feelings as opposed to just the words they are using. This may facilitate the development of rapport and trust.

Be empathetic and patient: People with dementia might need more time to comprehend information, therefore it's crucial to do so. Give them time to react, and refrain from interjecting.

Use visual aids: Objects or photos that are visually appealing can help those who have dementia understand what is being said. This is particularly beneficial when conveying complex information.

Minimize distractions: It's crucial to keep noise and other activities that can impede speech to a minimum when speaking with people who have dementia.

Use positive reinforcement: Positive reinforcement can help to foster positive interactions and enhance communication. It can take the form of praise or encouragement.

In summary, patience, understanding, and a willingness to adjust are necessary for effective communication with those who have dementia. These suggestions can help carers improve their communication abilities, encourage pleasant relationships, and raise the general quality of life for dementia patients.

Strategies for Dealing With Difficult Behaviors

Dealing with challenging behaviors can be one of the major difficulties for caregivers when providing care for people who have dementia. Communication and caregiving can be more difficult due to the changes that dementia can bring about in mood, conduct, and personality. Caregivers must recognize that these actions are a result of the sickness and must not be interpreted negatively. Instead, they should concentrate on creating plans to control these behaviors and raise the person's quality of life.

Agitation, hostility, roaming, and hallucinations are some typical challenging behaviors among people with dementia. Unmet needs, habitual changes, or environmental factors like loudness or overstimulation are just a few of the things that might cause these behaviors. Here are some tactics for handling challenging behaviors in people with dementia:

Identify and address the underlying cause: Difficult behaviors can come from unmet demands including hunger, thirst, pain, or discomfort. The basic requirements of the person with dementia should be satisfied, and caregivers should make sure they are comfortable.

Use distraction techniques: You can defuse a tense situation by diverting the person's attention to an activity or another subject. Simple pursuits like puzzle-solving, music-listening, and photo-viewing can successfully divert attention.

Use validation techniques: Validate and acknowledge the person's sentiments. This is paying attention to their worries and responding in a way that demonstrates empathy and comprehension. For instance, a caregiver might say, "I can tell that you're feeling frustrated. That must be difficult," in response to a dementia patient who is expressing displeasure.

Maintain a calm and reassuring demeanor: Dementia sufferers may get irritated or anxious if they perceive their caregiver to be upset or stressed. Even in trying circumstances, caregivers must maintain their composure and assurance.

Use positive reinforcement: This strategy rewards desired actions while ignoring or rerouting undesirable ones. For instance, if a dementia patient is engaging in wandering behavior, the caregiver may move their focus to another activity and encourage them when they do so.

Avoid arguments or confrontations: A person with dementia may become agitated if they feel challenged or contradicted, so avoid fights and confrontations. Instead of engaging in debates or confrontations, caregivers should strive to refocus the patient's attention or validate their sentiments.

Use non-verbal communication: Nonverbal cues like tone of voice, gestures, and facial expressions can be just as crucial as verbal cues. Caregivers should speak in a soothing, quiet tone of voice and refrain from making any violent or confrontational gestures or facial expressions.

Overall, managing challenging behaviors in people with dementia can be difficult, but employing these tactics can assist carers in doing so and enhance both the quality of life for the person with dementia and their caregiver.

Managing Caregiver Stress

The burden of providing care for a loved one who has dementia can be emotionally and physically taxing. The burden of the caregiver's duties can be great, and stress and burnout are frequent experiences for caregivers. To give their loved ones the greatest care possible, caregivers must put their health first. The following are some techniques for reducing caregiver stress:

Prioritize self-care: While taking care of a loved one who has dementia, caregivers frequently overlook their own needs. To reduce stress levels, it's crucial to give self-care top priority. This may include regularly participating in physical exercise, adhering to a healthy diet, and ensuring sufficient periods of rest. Also, caregivers should schedule time for hobbies they have, like reading, going on walks, or hanging out with friends.

Seek support: Providing care might be a lonely job, but it's crucial to remember that you're not alone. To get emotional support, turn to your loved ones and friends or think about joining an organization for caregivers. Support groups provide a secure setting where members can talk about their worries and feelings with others who are going through similar things.

Respite care: Respite care enables caregivers to take a break from their caregiving duties, providing them with some relief. Relatives can be taken to a respite care facility or a trained caregiver can visit them at home as part of respite care.

Practice stress-reducing techniques: Caregivers can utilize a variety of stress-relieving methods to control their levels of stress, including yoga, deep breathing, and meditation. These methods can assist in calming the mind and lowering stress and anxiety levels.

Take breaks: To refuel and look for themselves, caregivers must spend time away from their caregiving responsibilities. Spending time with friends or family, going for a little walk, or reading a book are a few examples of this. Also, caregivers should think about respite care choices, such as hiring a professional caregiver or asking a friend or family member to temporarily take over caregiving responsibilities.

Set boundaries: Carers frequently feel guilty for taking time off or declining additional caring duties. To prevent burnout and to make sure you have the time and energy to give your loved one the best care possible, it's crucial to establish limits.

Get professional help: If you are feeling stressed out and unable to control it, it may be good to do so. The stress of being a caretaker can be managed with the help and direction of a therapist or counselor, who can also help you feel better mentally overall. Also, your primary care physician might offer sources and recommendations for expert assistance.

Maintain a positive attitude: Carers should try to find joy in the time spent with their loved ones and concentrate on the good parts of caregiving. Finding pastimes for both the caregiver and the loved one, such as walking or listening to music, might help with this.

Taking care of legal and financial matters: Family caregivers need to make sure that the legal and financial affairs of their loved ones are in order. This may entail drafting a will or power of attorney, handling finances, and making sure the cherished one is properly insured.

CHAPTER FOUR

Creating a Safe and Supportive Environment

An essential component of dementia care is creating a secure and encouraging atmosphere. It entails altering the living situation to ensure the security and well-being of the dementia patient. Moreover, independence can be encouraged and accident and injury risk can be decreased in a secure and encouraging setting. In this chapter, we'll look at many tactics and adjustments that may be done to provide a secure and encouraging atmosphere for people with dementia.

Home Safety Considerations

Making the environment for people with dementia safe and supportive must take home safety into account. The living environment can be changed to lower the chance of accidents and injuries while fostering the independence of the dementia patient. The following are a few home safety recommendations for people with dementia:

Remove tripping hazards: Eliminate trip risks including loose carpeting, cluttered walkways, and electrical cables to prevent accidents. The risk of falls can be considerably decreased by removing these tripping hazards. Ensure sure the walkways are uncluttered and clear.

Install grab bars and handrails: Those with mobility difficulties can get assistance and stability from grab bars and handrails. They can reduce falls by being installed in stairways, hallways, and bathrooms.

Secure windows and doors: Dementia patients may wander or become disoriented and attempt to escape the property. A person with dementia can be kept safe by locking windows and doors to help stop them from roaming.

Remove or lock up potentially dangerous items: Lock away drugs, household supplies, and other potentially hazardous things. Eliminate them if possible. These items can be hazardous or even fatal if consumed by confused individuals with dementia.

Label and organize items: Items with labels and proper organization make it easier for people with dementia to find what they need and are less likely to become confused. They can locate items more quickly and readily if drawers and cabinets are labeled.

Provide adequate lighting: To avoid confusion and to reduce the danger of falls, provide appropriate lighting. Ensure that the living space is well-lit, particularly in high-risk areas like corridors and stairways.

In general, making these changes to your home can help you give people with dementia a safe and encouraging atmosphere.

Adapting the Living Environment for Dementia Patients

A key component of dementia care is adapting to the living situation. People with dementia can experience less anxiety, confusion, and disorientation by living in a secure and comforting environment. People with dementia can maintain their independence and quality of life by making little changes to their living environment.

The following are some recommendations for modifying the living situation for dementia patients:

Minimize clutter: For those with dementia, clutter can lead to confusion and distress. Simplify your living space by getting rid of extra objects and keeping only the necessities close at hand.

Install safety devices: Install safety equipment to stop falls and injuries, such as grab bars, handrails, and nonslip flooring. Install gates to block access to dangerous locations, and make sure the steps are well-lit.

Label items: Items with both written and visual labels can assist people with dementia identify and find necessary objects. Labeling the doors to various rooms and utilizing color-coded labels for various goods are some examples of how to do this.

Use familiar items: Utilizing recognizable items can make dementia sufferers feel more at ease and less nervous. Provide a sense of familiarity and lessen confusion by using comfortable bedding, furniture, and décor.

Simplify the environment: Reduce the environment's complexity since too much stimulus might overwhelm those with dementia. Reduce background distractions, reduce noise, and use relaxing colors and patterns to make your home more simple to live in.

Ensure adequate lighting: Make sure there is appropriate illumination because it might make dementia patients feel disoriented and confused. Make sure the living space is well-lit, either by bright natural light or artificial illumination. Employ nightlights to reduce the risk of falling and becoming lost at night.

Create a comfortable environment: Individuals with dementia may experience anxiety and confusion in strange settings. Use comforting sounds, smells, and other sensory clues to create a cozy atmosphere.

Careful consideration of the unique needs and preferences of those who have dementia is necessary when modifying the living environment. Dementia sufferers can keep their freedom and quality of life in a secure setting by making the necessary adjustments.

Managing Daily Routines

While managing daily routines for people with dementia can be difficult, it is a crucial part of dementia care. Routines can offer stability and structure, thereby easing agitation, disorientation, and worry. The objective is to create a routine that is predictable and regular while also catering to the requirements and preferences of the individual.

The following are some suggestions for directing daily activities for those with dementia:

Establish a routine: It's critical to establish a daily schedule that accommodates the person's requirements and preferences. The regimen should be well-organized but adaptable, allowing for adjustments as needed. Consistency is essential because it gives the person a sense of more control and lessens confusion and worry.

Simplify tasks: Simplify things by dividing them into smaller, more manageable steps to reduce the feeling of overload. Utilize reminders and visual clues to assist them remember what to do next. Put an image of a toothbrush next to the sink, for instance, to remind the person to brush their teeth.

Encourage independence: Promote independence by letting the person take care of as much as they can independently, even if it takes more time. Their freedom and self-esteem are maintained as a result. Where appropriate, offer help and support; nevertheless, avert taking entire control.

Plan activities: Choose activities that the person will find enjoyable and stimulating. This can involve socializing, exercising, and engaging in hobbies. Promote involvement in familiar and meaningful activities for them.

Use positive reinforcement: Provide positive reinforcement by praising the person for their efforts and successes, no matter how modest they may be. They gain more self-assurance as a result, and constructive conduct is reinforced.

Be flexible: Be aware that the person's requirements and capacities may evolve. Prepare to modify the routine if required to account for these changes.

Maintain a calm environment: Ensure that the surroundings are serene and distraction-free. This can facilitate relaxation and lessen tension and disorientation.

These suggestions can help caregivers provide people with dementia the structure and support they require to get through each day while also assisting them in maintaining a sense of independence and control.

Safety Tips for Outdoor Activities

For people with dementia, ensuring safety outdoors is essential since it can help avoid mishaps and injuries. Some safety advice for outdoor activities are provided below:

Keep a close eye on the individual: When engaging in outdoor activities, it's crucial to keep an eye on the person with dementia. Never let them be alone, and keep a tight check on them.

Choose safe and familiar locations: It is best to pick locations that the person is comfortable with and that are secure for them. For example, you could go for a stroll in the neighborhood park or visit a community center close by.

Wear appropriate clothing and footwear: Ensure sure the person is dressed correctly for the weather and activity, including the footwear they are wearing. Make sure their footwear is supportive, comfortable, and durable.

Utilize mobility aids: If a person with dementia needs a mobility aid, make sure they are using it correctly and that it is in good condition.

Avoid busy areas: It's advisable to stay away from places that are crowded or busy, as individuals with dementia might feel anxious or stressed out being in such environments. This can include places like busy shopping malls or crowded streets.

Be prepared for emergencies: Establish a plan in advance to deal with any potential emergencies. This can involve having a cell phone that is fully charged with you and knowing where the closest hospital or medical facility is.

Consider the time of day: To avoid the heat of the day, schedule outside activities for when it is cooler outside, such as early morning or late afternoon.

Stay alert for changes in behavior: Be alert for any behavioral changes, such as confusion or disorientation, and be ready to modify the activity if necessary.

Caregivers can ensure that outdoor activities for people with dementia are pleasurable and safe by adhering to these safety recommendations.

CHAPTER FIVE

Activities and Engagement for People with Dementia

The need for keeping people with dementia active and involved in worthwhile activities to support their physical, emotional, and cognitive well-being is emphasized in this chapter. The social isolation and boredom that can result from dementia can exacerbate cognitive decline symptoms and lower overall quality of life.

Among other advantages, participating in activities can aid with behavioral symptom reduction, mood improvement, and social interaction growth. This chapter will offer a variety of tactics and suggestions for games and engagement that will help people with dementia live more fully.

Importance Of Meaningful Activities

For those who have dementia, participating in worthwhile activities is crucial since it can enhance their general well-being and quality of life. A person's sense of purpose can be enhanced and feelings of isolation or loneliness can be diminished by engaging in meaningful activities that foster feelings of competence, self-esteem, and self-worth. Also, it can support the maintenance of mental and physical capacities throughout time.

Meaningful activities are those that are catered to the individual's interests, talents, and capabilities. For instance, someone who previously enjoyed gardening and has dementia may continue to take care of a modest garden and feel delight in doing so. Similar to this, someone who enjoys cooking may gain from performing basic kitchen activities like assembling a sandwich or whisking a batch of batter.

For those with dementia, meaningful activities can also be used as treatment. For instance, engaging people with dementia in worthwhile activities can be accomplished through the use of art therapy, music therapy, and pet therapy. These treatments can help with agitation, depression, and anxiety symptoms as well as communication, socializing, and emotional expression.

Making meaningful connections with the person with dementia can also provide family members and caregivers a chance to get to know them better. Family members and caregivers can improve communication, fortify their bonds, and make happy memories by engaging in activities together.

In general, dementia care must include participation in meaningful activities. It can raise self-esteem, foster possibilities for connection and growth, and enhance the quality of life for those who are living with dementia.

Strategies for Planning Activities

Making meaningful plans for those who have dementia can enhance their quality of life, retain their physical and mental capabilities, and lessen their symptoms of melancholy and worry. Listed below are a few methods for organizing activities for people with dementia:

Take into account their abilities and interests: It's critical to design activities that are specific to each person's skills and passions. This can ensure that the activity is fun and interesting for them while also encouraging feelings of success and fulfillment.

Keep it simple: It's crucial to plan activities that are clear and simple to understand. In addition to making it simpler for the person with dementia to join and engage in the activity, this can also help to lessen irritation and confusion.

Provide visual cues: Assist people with dementia in understanding and participating in activities by providing visual cues. For more difficult tasks, this could entail giving step-by-step directions or using illustrations or diagrams to illustrate the process.

Use reminiscence therapy: Reminiscence therapy entails enticing people to discuss their earlier experiences and memories. As it can support the development of a feeling of identity and self-worth, this can be a useful strategy for including people with dementia in meaningful activities.

Focus on the process, not the outcome: It's crucial to pay attention to the activity's process rather than the outcome. The objective is to involve the person with dementia in a worthwhile and enjoyable activity rather than to create a flawless final product.

Incorporate sensory stimulation: Activities that include sensory stimulation might be especially captivating for people who have dementia. This could involve activities like watching art, listening to music, or engaging in tactile hobbies like gardening.

Provide social opportunities: Socialization can be a key component of meaningful activities. Possibilities for social engagement can aid in lowering feelings of loneliness and fostering sentiments of connection and belonging.

Be flexible: Plan activities for people with dementia with flexibility in mind because their interests and abilities may vary over time. Activities can stay engaging and pleasurable for the individual if you are willing to adjust and change them as necessary.

Building Social Connections

Maintaining a person's quality of life while living with dementia requires them to develop social relationships. It is essential for people living with dementia to feel socially active and connected to their friends, family, and community. Sadly, speech problems, memory loss, and other cognitive impairments cause people with dementia to often feel socially isolated and withdraw from social activities. This may result in isolation, despair, and a deterioration of general health.

So, it is crucial to assist those who are living with dementia in creating and sustaining social bonds. Encouragement of involvement in socialization-promoting activities and occasions, such as group outings, neighborhood gatherings, and leisure pursuits, is one tactic. These pursuits can foster interpersonal relationships and enhance mental and physical health.

Involving family members and friends in the care and support of people with dementia is very crucial. In addition to encouraging visitors from family and friends, caregivers can help the dementia patient and their loved ones communicate. Through the use of video chats, social media, and online support groups, technology can also be used to enhance social contact and communication.

In addition, it's critical to create a welcoming and inclusive environment for dementia sufferers in the neighborhood. This can entail planning accessible, inviting, and supportive events and environments for people with dementia. As a result of these initiatives, dementia sufferers may have more chances to interact socially with like-minded others and take part in activities that are meaningful to them.

In general, fostering social relationships is crucial for improving dementia patients' quality of life. It is crucial to promote engagement in socialization-enhancing activities, include family members and friends in the care and support of those with dementia, and create a welcoming and accepting environment in the community. People with dementia can carry on with meaningful activities and keep their feeling of self and belonging by putting social connections first.

CHAPTER SIX

Resources and Help for Caregivers

Taking care of a loved one who has dementia can be difficult and demanding. To preserve their health and wellness, caregivers may face stress, weariness, and burnout. As a result, they may require help and support. Fortunately, several tools and programs can assist carers in overcoming the difficulties of dementia caregiving.

We will look at some of the resources and options for assistance that are available to caregivers in this chapter, including support groups, respite care, and counseling services. We will also go through how caregivers may prioritize self-care, manage their own mental and physical health, and take care of themselves.

Support Groups and Counseling Services

Caregiver resources like support groups and counseling are crucial for dementia patients. Support groups and counseling services can offer a secure and encouraging environment where caregivers can connect with others who are going through similar experiences and receive emotional support, education, and useful advice. Providing care for an individual with dementia can be a challenging and solitary experience.

Several types of support groups are available, including face-to-face gatherings, online discussion boards, and phone conferences. They could be led by trained volunteers, medical professionals, or other caretakers. While some support groups are more general and cover a variety of dementia caregiving-related subjects, others could concentrate on particular problems like controlling difficult behaviors, navigating the healthcare system, or dealing with loss and bereavement.

Mental health specialists like psychologists, social workers, or certified counselors may offer counseling services. Counseling can be provided individually or in groups, and it can address a variety of problems, such as the strain on caregivers, sadness, anxiety, and sorrow. The person with dementia and their family members may also be able to get counseling services to help them deal with the emotional effects of the condition and negotiate the adjustments and difficulties it brings.

Support groups and counseling services can provide a range of benefits for caregivers, including:

Emotional support: Connecting with people who can relate to their struggles and share them helps caregivers feel less alone and more a part of the community.

Education and information: Support groups and counseling programs can give caregivers knowledge about dementia, its symptoms, and its progression, as well as techniques for managing the illness and taking care of their loved ones.

Practical advice and resources: Carers can learn about tools and resources that can assist them manage their caring duties and support the dementia patient.

Coping skills: To effectively manage stress, anxiety, and other emotional difficulties brought on by providing dementia care, caregivers can learn practical coping mechanisms.

Validation and affirmation: By receiving validation and affirmation for the crucial and frequently challenging work they undertake, caregivers might feel less guilt, worry, and self-doubt.

Several community organizations, healthcare practitioners, and online resources offer access to support groups and counseling services. To get the most out of these tools, caregivers should pick a support group or counseling program that fits their unique needs and preferences and join frequently.

Respite Care Options

Taking care of a loved one who has dementia can be difficult and demanding. Carers frequently take on various responsibilities, ranging from giving emotional support to overseeing medical treatment and performing everyday chores. There may not be much time left over for self-care and other activities as a result of this being emotionally, psychologically, and physically draining. For carers to take a break from their caregiving responsibilities and concentrate on their well-being, respite care is a crucial resource.

Short-term, emergency care services are referred to as respite care, and they are meant to relieve the burden of primary caregivers. Respite care can take several forms, including in-home care, adult day care, and short-term residential care. Depending on their requirements and preferences, a caregiver and their loved one will benefit most from a certain sort of respite care.

As the care recipient stays in the comfort of their own home, in-home respite care offers the caregiver momentary relief. Along with helping with daily tasks like getting dressed, bathing, and preparing meals, in-home care workers can also offer companionship and social interaction.

Another alternative for respite care is adult day care, which enables carers to take a break while their loved one is looked after and supervised during the day. Adult daycare facilities provide a variety of services, such as food, activities, chances for social interaction, and medical supervision.

Family and friends can also offer respite care, but it's crucial to make sure that both the caregiver and the person with dementia receiving care are satisfied with the arrangement.

Caregivers can get in touch with neighborhood residential care facilities, adult day care centers, and home care organizations to get access to respite care. Also, some businesses and government initiatives provide financial support for respite care services.

In general, respite care is a crucial tool for dementia caregivers to avoid burnout and maintain their health and well-being. It enables caregivers to take a break and refuel so they can keep giving their loved ones the best care possible.

Financial Assistance and Legal Resources

Providing care for someone who has dementia may be an expensive and complicated procedure that calls for careful supervision and planning. When they attempt to navigate the complex healthcare system and match their loved one's needs with their financial obligations, many caregivers encounter financial and legal difficulties. Fortunately, there are several tools at their disposal to assist carers in navigating the financial and legal facets of dementia care.

Financial support for caregivers may include:

Medicare and Medicaid: Both offer financial support for healthcare costs, such as those associated with long-term care, hospital stays, prescription drugs, and doctor visits. For those who are over 65 or have certain disabilities, Medicare offers an option. Low-income individuals who satisfy specific eligibility requirements can get Medicaid.

Social Security Disability Insurance (SSDI) and Supplemental Security Income (SSI): Both the Social Security Disability Insurance (SSDI) and Supplemental Security Income (SSI) programs offer financial support to low-income individuals with impairments. While SSI is available to low-income individuals with disabilities who have not worked or paid Social Security taxes, SSDI is only available to those who have worked and paid Social Security taxes.

Veterans benefits: Veterans and their spouses may be qualified for a range of benefits, including healthcare, disability payments, pensions, and retirement benefits. Additionally, certain veterans can be qualified for aid and attendance benefits, which cover the cost of long-term care.

Legal resources for caregivers may include:

Elder law attorneys: These lawyers focus on aging-related legal matters, such as Medicaid planning, long-term care planning, and estate planning.

Advance directives: Advance directives are legal documents that let people decide in advance how they'll be treated for their medical needs and final days. Do-not-resuscitate orders, medical powers of attorney, and living wills are a few examples of these documents.

Guardianship and conservatorship: To make legal choices on behalf of their loved ones who have dementia, caregivers in some circumstances may need to apply for guardianship or conservatorship.

The Alzheimer's Association, the Family Caregiver Alliance, and regional senior centers are just a few examples of local and national organizations where caregivers can get assistance and services. To assist carers in managing the numerous difficulties associated with dementia care, these organizations can offer knowledge, instruction, and support. In addition, many communities provide respite care services, which give carers a little break from their caregiving obligations by offering care and support.

Ultimately, carers should look into all of their options to get the help they require to manage their own financial and legal obligations while still giving their loved ones with dementia the high-quality care they require.

Planning for the Future

Caregiving for a loved one with dementia requires careful planning for the future. The dementia patient will probably need additional care and support as the disease worsens, so it's critical to have a plan in place to make sure their requirements are addressed. These are some important things to think about when making plans:

Advance care planning: This involves talking about and writing down a person's medical preferences and end-of-life care preferences. Decisions about resuscitation, comfort care, and life-sustaining therapies can fall under this category. These discussions should start early, and you should keep them updated as the person's health evolves.

Legal planning: Legal planning involves making sure that the person with dementia has the legal documentation necessary to uphold their rights and defend their preferences. This could include a living will, a durable power of attorney for finances and healthcare, as well as a will or trust.

Financial planning: It's crucial to consider the person with dementia's financial needs because their care may become increasingly expensive. This could entail establishing a long-term care insurance policy, investigating government benefits like Medicaid or veterans' benefits, and locating additional sources of assistance like neighborhood initiatives or nonprofit groups.

Housing and care options: When dementia patients' care requirements vary, it's critical to take their housing and care options into account. This can entail looking into facilities for assisted living or nursing homes as well as in-home care alternatives like home health aides or respite care.

While establishing plans, it's crucial to include the person with dementia as much as possible in the decision-making process while also being honest about their capabilities and limitations. Also, it's critical to periodically review the plan and make any necessary modifications in light of the person's evolving requirements and circumstances.

CHAPTER SEVEN

End-of-Life Care for People with Dementia

When facing the difficulties of caring for someone with dementia, family, and caregivers should talk about end-of-life care for those with the condition. Since that dementia is a degenerative illness that can ultimately result in death, it's crucial to maintain the patient's comfort, dignity, and quality of life throughout this terminal phase. A patient's comfort and symptom control should be the main goals of the end-of-life care plan.

This chapter will examine the numerous facets of end-of-life care for dementia patients, including the functions of palliative care, hospice care, and advanced care planning.

Understanding End-Of-Life Care

Care provided to those who are suffering from a terminal illness or condition is referred to as "end-of-life care." End-of-life care can be particularly difficult for those who have dementia. Dementia is a degenerative and irreversible disease that can eventually impair one's capacity to interact with others, remember familiar faces, and do routine everyday tasks.

To make sure that their loved ones receive the proper care and support throughout their final phases, families and caregivers must be aware of the alternatives for end-of-life care for individuals with dementia.

Hospice and Palliative Care Options

For patients with dementia, there are two options for end-of-life care: hospice and palliative care. These solutions are meant to control the patient's symptoms and offer both the patient and their family members emotional support.

Those with a terminal illness and a prognosis of six months or fewer to live are typically given hospice care. Hospice care is often given to patients in their homes, although it can also be given in a hospice center. The primary goals of hospice care are to maximize the patient's level of comfort, control their pain and symptoms, and offer the patient's family members emotional and spiritual support. The patient's carers may receive respite care through hospice care.

People with serious illnesses, such as dementia, can get palliative care at any stage of their condition. Palliative care focuses on symptom management and enhancing the patient's quality of life. Also, it offers the patient's family members and themselves spiritual and emotional support. Palliative care can be given at a hospital, hospice, or the patient's home.

A group of medical experts, such as doctors, nurses, social workers, and chaplains, can offer both hospice and palliative care. To give the patient and their family members the best care possible, these professionals collaborate.

Early on in the dementia journey, family members and caregivers must discuss end-of-life care options with the patient's medical team. This can assist guarantee that the patient's preferences are honored and that the proper treatment is given when it's needed.

Advance Care Planning

The end-of-life care provided to dementia patients must include advanced care planning. It entails talking about and writing down a person's wishes for medical procedures and treatments in case they lose the ability to make those decisions for themselves. People can make decisions that are in line with their values and preferences thanks to advance care planning, which gives them a sense of dignity and control.

Advanced care planning for those with dementia entails many crucial steps. They include:

Initiate conversations: Family members and caregivers should start a conversation with the dementia patient about their goals, values, and preferences for end-of-life care. These conversations must take place frequently and early so that the person can express their choices and have their requests respected.

Choose a healthcare proxy: If a person with dementia loses the ability to make decisions about their health, a healthcare proxy can act on their behalf. The person should pick a companion they can trust and who shares their values.

Complete advance directives: Advance directives are legal agreements that outline a person's wishes for medical care, including whether they want life-sustaining therapies and when they do. These legal forms include durable powers of attorney for healthcare and living wills.

Advance directives must be routinely reviewed and updated to ensure that they still reflect the person's preferences. Advance care planning necessitates excellent communication with healthcare professionals, such as doctors and nurses. The patient's choices and directives should be noted in their medical record, and healthcare professionals should be aware of their desires.

Especially in the case of dementia, advanced care planning can be difficult for families and caregivers. Yet it's crucial to make sure that the person's wishes are honored and that they receive the right care as they approach death. Healthcare professionals, social workers, and attorneys are just a few of the options that can help with advance care planning.

Coping with Grief and Loss

A crucial part of providing end-of-life care for dementia patients is helping them deal with their grief and loss. The progressive loss of a loved one's personality, memories, and capacity for effective communication when they have dementia can make grief more difficult. When they see their loved one deteriorate, caregivers may feel a sense of loss and grief. They may also feel anticipatory grief as they get ready for their loved one's eventual death.

Caregivers must have help during this trying time. There are numerous options accessible, such as bereavement therapy, support groups, and internet discussion boards. Talking to people who have gone through a similar experience and can provide empathy and understanding may be helpful for caregivers.

In addition to seeking support, caregivers can take steps to cope with their grief and loss. This may include self-care activities such as exercise, meditation, and spending time with friends and family. Caregivers may also find it helpful to create a memory book or other keepsake that celebrates their loved one's life and accomplishments.

Caregivers must understand that grieving is a normal and natural component of the dying process. Caregivers who seek support and look after themselves will be better able to deal with their feelings of loss and grief and give their loved one with dementia the best care possible.

CHAPTER EIGHT

Innovative Approaches to Dementia Care

Innovative dementia care strategies employ novel and imaginative techniques to raise the standard of living for those who have the disease. These strategies can aid in addressing some of the difficulties that people with dementia and those who care for them confront, such as behavioral issues, communication difficulties, and social isolation.

As opposed to a one-size-fits-all strategy, person-centered care, which emphasizes the individual's particular needs and preferences, is a goal of innovative approaches. This chapter will look at some of the cutting-edge methods that have been developed recently, such as technology-based therapies, music therapy, recollection therapy, art therapy, and music therapy.

Emerging Technologies for Dementia Care

To improve the quality of life for those who have dementia, their caregivers, and family members, emerging technologies are being created and put into practice to improve dementia care. Here are a few of the cutting-edge technologies being investigated or used for dementia care:

Ambient Assisted Living (AAL): Ambient Assisted Living (AAL) is the use of smart home gadgets and other technologies to support and help individuals with dementia while also assuring their safety and security. The use of voice-activated gadgets for reminders, medication dispensers, and sensors to detect falls or wandering are examples of this.

Virtual Reality (VR): VR can be utilized to give dementia patients immersive experiences like virtual travel or recollection therapy. Additionally, it can be applied to cognitive stimulation activities like memory games and workouts.

Robotics: Robotics can benefit people with dementia in several ways, such as by reimbursing them for taking their medications, assisting with movement, and offering companionship. Robots can also track vital indicators and notify caretakers of any emergencies.

Artificial Intelligence (AI) : With artificial intelligence (AI), it is possible to examine vast volumes of data and identify early indications of dementia or forecast future decline. Personalized care plans and better drug management can also be created using it.

Wearable devices: Wearable devices, such as smartwatches or activity trackers, may keep an eye on your heart rate, blood pressure, and other vital signals. Using this information, carers can keep an eye on and manage the health of dementia patients.

Telehealth: Telehealth refers to the use of technology to deliver medical support and care remotely. This can involve connecting with medical professionals virtually, keeping an eye on health concerns remotely, and having access to internet information and support networks.

The quality of life for dementia patients and their caretakers could potentially be improved by these cutting-edge technologies. Yet, it's crucial to guarantee that these technologies are user-friendly, accessible, and used in a way that respects the dignity and autonomy of the dementia patient. It is crucial to understand that these technologies should be utilized in conjunction with human connection and care, not in place of it.

Person-Centered Care Approaches

Person-centered care is a kind of dementia treatment that focuses on identifying and addressing the unique needs of the dementia patient. The method acknowledges that every person is different and has a unique set of preferences, skills, and life experiences. It seeks to advance the quality of life, independence, and dignity of those who have dementia.

Dementia care can be based on some person-centered care tenets which include:

Respect the person's individuality: Respect for the individual's uniqueness entails getting to know the person and learning about their preferences, interests, and life experiences. With this data, a care strategy that is suited to their particular need can be developed.

Empower the dementia patient: Person-centered care encourages dementia patients to take an active role in their treatment and to maintain as much independence as possible. Offering options for daily routines, activities, and meals may be one way to do this.

Create a supportive environment: To create a supportive atmosphere, you must first create a secure, familiar, and comfortable physical and social setting. It could entail modifying the surroundings to better suit the person's requirements, for as by adding grab bars or taking away trip risks.

Focus on the person's strengths: Person-centered care acknowledges that individuals with dementia still possess strengths and abilities that can be developed and maintained. This could entail finding ways to encourage communication and socializing or providing the individual with activities they enjoy.

Involve family and caregivers: Person-centered care emphasizes the crucial part that the family and the carers play in assisting people with dementia. They must be given assistance and education, and they must be included in the planning of their care.

A paradigm shift from a disease-focused model to a person-focused model is necessary to implement person-centered care. Both individual attitudes and actions may need to change, as well as the culture and procedures of care organizations. Yet, studies have demonstrated that person-centered care can boost caregiver job satisfaction while also enhancing the quality of life for those with dementia.

Future Directions In Dementia Care

Globally, public health concerns about dementia are steadily expanding. Every year, more people are diagnosed with dementia, and by 2050, that number is projected to have tripled. Finding new methods of dementia care is therefore urgently needed. There have been many interesting advancements in dementia care over the past few years, and many researchers and professionals think that these breakthroughs have a bright future ahead of them.

The use of technology in dementia care is one of the most important future directions. The development and application of technology-based therapies to support dementia patients and their caregivers are abundantly possible thanks to technological advancement. To assist persons with dementia to live more freely and safely, there are smart houses that make use of sensors and smart technology. Also, there are video games and virtual reality experiences made to excite the mind and body and lower the risk of cognitive decline.

The growing emphasis on individualized, person-centered care methods is a fascinating trend in dementia care. Person-centered care, which supports the needs, preferences, and values of the person with dementia, centers care around that individual. It acknowledges the individuality of each person living with dementia and their range of abilities and needs. The person-centered approach to care emphasizes treating the person with dementia as an individual with a special history, personality, and identity rather than just as a patient with a diagnosis.

Another interesting area for dementia treatment in the future is the development of non-pharmacological interventions. The goal of non-pharmacological therapies is to enhance the quality of life and lessen dementia symptoms without the use of drugs. Music therapy, art therapy, pet therapy, and recollection therapy are a few non-pharmacological therapies. The quality of life for dementia patients and their caregivers may be significantly impacted by these therapies.

Lastly, there is a growing understanding that dementia is a public health problem that necessitates a thorough, multi-sectoral response. To address the complex issues related to dementia, there will be a need for increased cooperation between government organizations, community organizations, and health and social care providers in the future. For this strategy to improve the level of care and support for those with dementia and their families, more money will need to be allocated for dementia research, public awareness initiatives, and legislation changes.

Dementia is a complicated and difficult affliction, but there is hope for the future. The future of dementia care looks bright thanks to emerging technologies, person-centered care strategies, non-pharmacological therapies, and collaborative care paradigms. The lives of millions of people with dementia and their families might be improved with continuous research, innovation, and funding.

CHAPTER NINE

Cultural Considerations in Dementia Care

Understanding dementia needs not just familiarity with the condition but also respect for the person's and their family's cultural heritage and religious beliefs. The way dementia is viewed and handled, as well as how care is given, can be significantly impacted by cultural values and beliefs. This chapter will examine the cultural factors that must be taken into account while caring for a person who has dementia as well as the ways that cultural practices and beliefs can be incorporated into dementia care.

Understanding Cultural Diversity in Dementia Care

To provide appropriate and effective care for people from varied origins, one must have a thorough understanding of cultural diversity in dementia care. People of various races, religions, and cultures can develop dementia, and being aware of the cultural characteristics of dementia can aid with communication, lessen stigma, and enhance care results.

Language, ideas, values, traditions, rituals, and family systems are only a few examples of the many aspects of cultural variety. For instance, while dementia may be stigmatized in some cultures, it may not be in others, where it may be perceived as a shameful affliction. Decisions about care, including choices for alternative or traditional medicine, may also be influenced by cultural views and values.

It is crucial to understand that cultural variety is not just confined to racial or ethnic differences. Other elements including gender, sexual preference, social standing, and place of residence can also have an impact on culture. Caretakers should be conscious of these elements and make an effort to comprehend each person's particular cultural background and preferences.

People and their families must be included in care planning and decision-making to deliver care that is culturally appropriate. This can involve enquiring about cultural norms and practices surrounding health and disease as well as comparing and contrasting choices for care and treatment. Educating caregivers and workers about cultural diversity and fostering an environment of respect and tolerance are also vital.

Also, it could be beneficial to have employees or volunteers that share the same cultural heritage as the people being served. This can make communication easier and help to overcome cultural differences. To ensure successful communication, interpreters or translation services could also be required.

Ultimately, to deliver high-quality, person-centered dementia care, one must comprehend and appreciate cultural diversity. Caregivers can enhance effective care and raise the standard of living for dementia patients and their families by identifying and addressing cultural differences.

Challenges in Providing Culturally Sensitive Care

The importance of cultural variety in contemporary communities and its importance in dementia care cannot be overstated. The particular requirements of varied cultures make it difficult to provide culturally responsive treatment. Language obstacles, cultural prejudices, and cultural biases are a few of the difficulties in providing dementia patients with care that is sensitive to their cultural backgrounds.

One of the biggest obstacles to providing culturally sensitive treatment is language problems. The demands and preferences of patients may be difficult for caregivers who do not know their language. Caregiving requires effective communication, and poor communication can result in miscommunication and inadequate care.

Providing culturally responsive treatment can be extremely difficult due to cultural biases and assumptions. Caregivers who have preconceived notions about a certain cultural group may find it challenging to comprehend the individual requirements and preferences of their patients. This could result in unsuitable treatment and a lack of empathy. Similar to this, cultural prejudices might affect how well care is given. In other cases, caregivers may have a lack of respect for the patient's culture and beliefs because they perceive specific cultural customs or beliefs as archaic or primitive.

How care is given may also be affected by variations in cultural attitudes toward dementia and aging. While dementia may be stigmatized or seen as a normal part of aging in some cultures, it may also be taboo in others. These disparities in viewpoints may affect how relatives and caregivers approach providing care for a dementia patient.

Overall, recognizing the particular requirements and preferences of varied cultures is necessary to provide culturally sensitive care for people with dementia. Caregivers must be open-minded, non-judgmental, and willing to learn about various cultures. By overcoming these obstacles, caregivers can deliver efficient, compassionate care that honors the patient's dignity and cultural heritage.

Strategies for Providing Culturally Appropriate Care

It is crucial to provide dementia patients with care that is attentive to their cultural ideas and values by providing care that is culturally appropriate. The following are techniques that carers can use to deliver care that is appropriate for their culture:

Develop cultural competence: Developing cultural competence requires that caregivers spend time learning about the patient's cultural heritage. This entails comprehending their traditions, values, and worldview. With this understanding, carers can modify their caregiving style to be more courteous and sensitive to cultural differences.

Use culturally sensitive communication: Communication that is attentive to cultural differences is important when providing dementia care. The language used by caregivers should be precise, succinct, and culturally appropriate. Using culturally relevant non-verbal cues like body language and eye contact is also crucial.

Involve the family: In many cultures, relatives are crucial to the care of their loved ones who are suffering from dementia. Family members should be included in the care process, and caregivers should get their advice on how to best care for patients while respecting their cultural beliefs.

Adapt the care environment: The care environment should be modified to take the patient's cultural demands into account. This includes modifying the care environment's décor, music, and cuisine to reflect the patient's cultural heritage.

Address spirituality and religion: Discuss spirituality and religion: Several civilizations place a high value on spirituality and religion. The patient's spiritual and religious views should be respected by caregivers, who should also find methods to incorporate these values into the patient's care plan.

Be aware of cultural differences in the expression of dementia symptoms: Observe cultural variations in how dementia symptoms are expressed because they can vary from one culture to another. To prevent miscommunications and deliver proper care, caregivers should be aware of these cultural variations.

Seek cultural consultation: When in doubt, caregivers can get advice from cultural experts, such as clergymen or community leaders who are familiar with the patient's culture. They can offer perceptions of cultural values and customs that can help the caregiver deliver care that is suitable for their culture.

In summary, offering culturally competent treatment necessitates sensitivity, familiarity with, and comprehension of the patient's cultural background. Patient's quality of life will probably be improved by caregivers who can adapt their methods of care to be more courteous and sensitive to cultural differences.

Building Cultural Competence Among Caregivers

Developing cultural competence among caregivers is a crucial part of giving dementia patients culturally appropriate care. People from different cultural backgrounds can receive more effective and courteous care from caregivers who are aware of cultural diversity.

The following techniques can be used to increase cultural competency in caregivers:

Education and training: Training and education regarding cultural diversity, as well as the particular requirements and preferences of people from different cultures, should be given to caregivers. Workshops, seminars, and online courses on subjects like cultural humility, cultural competency, and communication techniques for dealing with people from different backgrounds can fall under this category.

Understanding cultural values: Caregivers should make an effort to comprehend the cultural values and beliefs of their patients and their families. Learning about their cultural heritage, traditions, and rituals and how these may affect their expectations and preferences for care can help with this. To offer treatment in a culturally acceptable way, caregivers might also interview patients and their families about their cultural beliefs and practices.

Cultural self-awareness: Caregivers should become aware of their cultural prejudices and presumptions, as well as how they may affect how they engage with clients and their families. To do this, they may need to consider how their cultural background, experiences, and beliefs may differ from those of their clients. Also, caregivers should be receptive to criticism and ready to alter their strategy as necessary.

Flexibility and adaptability: Carers should be prepared to modify their approach to providing care to accommodate the requirements and preferences of their clients from a variety of cultural backgrounds. To do this, it may be necessary to be adaptable to routines and schedules, include cultural customs and practices in caregiving activities, and use alternate communication tools like interpreters or translated materials.

Cooperation and partnership: To create a care plan that takes the clients' cultural values and preferences into consideration, caregivers should partner with clients and their families. This may entail consulting with clients and their families to get their views and participation in the selection of their care. To make sure that every part of care is culturally appropriate, caregivers should collaborate closely with other members of the care team, including interpreters, cultural liaisons, and medical professionals.

Caregivers can increase their cultural competence and give dementia patients from various cultural backgrounds more effective and respectful care by incorporating these strategies into their care approach.

CONCLUSION

In conclusion, providing care for those who have dementia can be a difficult and complex endeavor that calls for a variety of knowledge, skills, and resources. This guide has offered a thorough overview of the various facets of dementia care, including communication techniques, setting up a secure environment, managing daily routines, involving dementia patients in meaningful activities, accessing caregiver resources and support, end-of-life care, cutting-edge dementia care techniques, and cultural considerations.

To establish trust, create connections, and control difficult behaviors, effective communication is essential when providing care for people who have dementia. To encourage pleasant connections and facilitate communication with people who have dementia, caregivers can employ a variety of tactics, including active listening, nonverbal communication, and validation procedures.

To minimize accidents and injuries, encourage independence, and improve the quality of life for those with dementia, it is also crucial to create a safe and supportive atmosphere. Assistive gadgets can be used by caregivers to support daily living tasks as well as a variety of home safety measures, and living arrangements that are tailored to the needs of dementia patients.

Another essential component of dementia care is managing daily routines, which can help people with dementia maintain a feeling of routine and normalcy, avoid confusion and agitation, and improve both physical and emotional well-being. To assist people with dementia with their everyday tasks, caregivers can utilize several tactics, including creating routines, utilizing visual aids, and giving basic and understandable directions.

It's crucial to involve dementia sufferers in worthwhile activities since doing so can foster social relationships, preserve cognitive and physical function, and improve quality of life. Reminiscence therapy, music therapy, and art therapy are just a few of the inventive and cutting-edge techniques caregivers can employ to involve dementia patients in pleasurable and meaningful activities.

For caregivers to successfully manage the physical, emotional, and financial difficulties of caregiving, they must have access to caregiver support and resources. To cope with the demands of caregiving, caregivers can get assistance from a variety of sources, including support groups, counseling services, and respite care choices.

Because people with dementia frequently have complex physical and emotional demands as they approach the end of their lives, end-of-life care is also a crucial factor in dementia care. Advance care planning, hospice and palliative care alternatives, and coping techniques for grief and loss are all tools caregivers can use to assist people with dementia and their families during this difficult time.

New dementia care strategies including developing technologies, person-centered care, and non-pharmacological therapies are also encouraging ways to raise the standard of dementia care. These methods can improve the mental, emotional, and social health of dementia patients and the caregivers who care for them.

Individuals with dementia come from a variety of cultural origins, and they may have particular ideas, attitudes, and behaviors around health and illness. As a result, cultural concerns are crucial in dementia treatment. To provide dementia patients and their families with culturally sensitive care, caregivers might employ tactics like cultural awareness, cultural humility, and cultural competency.

In general, caring for someone with dementia necessitates a multidimensional strategy that attends to their physical, emotional, social, and cultural needs. Caregivers can improve the quality of life and deliver efficient and compassionate care to those with dementia by utilizing a variety of techniques and tools.

Printed in Great Britain
by Amazon

25717507R00056